The WetFeet Insider Guide to Negotiating Your Salary and Perks

2004 Edition

NOV 2004

Helping you make smarter career decisions.

WetFeet Inc.

609 Mission Street

Suite 400

San Francisco, CA 94105

Phone: (415) 284-7900 or 1-800-926-4JOB

Fax: (415) 284-7910

E-mail: info@wetfeet.com

Website: www.wetfeet.com

The WetFeet Insider Guide to Negotiating Your Salary and Perks

By Robert A. Fish, PhD

ISBN: 1-58207-252-3

Table of Contents

Negotiating Salary and Perks at a Glance

What Negotiation Can Do for You

- Give you job satisfaction—instead of job dissatisfaction
- Increase your credibility
- Get you a job offer that reflects your strengths

Build Your Bargaining Power

- Help the employer recognize the job's importance
- Make sure the employer sees you as the best candidate
- Suggest a short-term assignment to increase your bargaining power
- Negotiate with the right person—the decision-maker

Knowledge Makes a Difference

- Know what's most important to you
- Research the going rate for the job
- Determine what's negotiable and what's not
- Investigate potentially negotiable benefits beyond salary

Take Control

- Avoid being the first to suggest a salary
- Know how to get an offer
- Plan your reaction to the offer
- Be prepared to respond to the employer's negotiating tactics
- Keep your cool

Make an Informed Decision

- Go over your decision criteria
- Develop your best alternative prospect
- Know when to say no
- Know when to say yes
- Get it in writing

Getting Started

- Overview

- The Bottom Line

- Building Bargaining Power

Overview

You've jumped through all the hoops. You've developed a great resume, identi-fied a promising job opportunity, performed well in rounds of interviews, and now the call has finally come: They want you. Congratulations!

But wait—the most challenging part of your job search is still to come.It's time to negotiate your compensation and working conditions.

If you're in a strong position—lots of offers, outstanding technical skills, little competition—negotiating may be a matter of naming your price. Even so, strategy is important. You want your manager and coworkers to be glad to have you, not resentful of your demands.

Besides, few of us are this fortunate. The typical candidate really wants the job, is terrified of losing it by being too aggressive, and doesn't negotiate effec-tively—if at all. This Insider Guide aims to replace that fear with confidence. It will show you how to improve your standing with the employer, equip you with tools to assess your position and determine negotiating priorities, discuss a range of potential negotiating points, demonstrate how to handle a variety of situations, and prepare you to field the tough questions.

Whether this is your first job offer or your tenth, you'll do yourself a favor by honing your negotiation skills. Whatever the firm's initial offer is, it can often be improved—in many cases dramatically—through savvy negotiating. And once you're on the job, it'll be difficult to get the same boost, even with stellar performance.

This Insider takes you step by step through a negotiation process that will leave both you and your employer satisfied. The process begins much earlier than you may realize—with building a strong starting position. Your confidence, the way you present yourself, and how you discuss the job are all part of your negotiations. If you've become the clear top candidate for a position, you obviously have more bargaining power than if you appear little better than the next-best candidate. By the time you get to the bargaining table, a lot of your negotiating has already been accomplished—for better or worse.

Already at that point? Don't worry. We'll show you how to assess your bargaining position—whatever it is—and use negotiating tactics to get your best possible job offer. Maybe you can improve your salary by 5 percent or 20 percent. Maybe you can negotiate an early review with a raise for strong performance. And then there are bonuses, increased commission, stock options, educational benefits, extra vacation days, and a flexible work schedule. These and a host of other factors could mean the difference between job satisfaction and early discontent.

WetFeet®

The Bottom Line

Your time is one of your most valuable possessions. And when you take a job, you are giving up most of your waking hours to help others achieve their objectives. Isn't it worth investing a little time up front to make sure you're compensated at your full value?

Practice the techniques described in this Insider, do the research to back up your requests, and you can negotiate an excellent compensation package—not just a salary, but your other must-haves as well, and even a few nice-to-have items. If you do this well, your employer will also be pleased with the agreement—and even more impressed with you. Note that the principles here also apply to negotiating a raise, winning a coveted job assignment, reaching agreements with coworkers, and many other situations on and off the job.

Building Bargaining Power

Successful negotiation requires both strategic and tactical thinking. Strategy is the foundation—what you do to ensure that your bargaining position is as strong as it can be—and you should start working on it well before you sit down to hammer out the details with your future employer. Tactics are what you do to achieve the best outcome considering your bargaining position.

A well-thought-out strategy will make the most of your talents, education, job experiences, and recommendations, while neutralizing your limitations. In short, it will build your bargaining power.

So how do you develop a negotiating strategy? Let the following 11 principles be your guide.

1. Bargaining power is key.

2. Your bargaining power reflects the company's experiences with you.

3. The earlier you enter the hiring process, the more influence you have.

4. Taking on a short-term project can dramatically improve your bargaining power.

5. Know the market and develop alternative job offers.

6. Establish your priorities, and evaluate offers accordingly.

7. Be aware of what the employer can offer.

8. Assess your power position realistically.

9. Never be the first to name a salary.

10. Always negotiate with the decision maker.

11. Try to create situations that benefit you and the company.

1. Bargaining power is key.

Bargaining power is what you have if there's an oil field on fire and you're the only outfit able to be on the scene smothering the flames tomorrow. Bargaining power is what you have if you wrote the year's hottest-selling business title, and now every company wants you as a speaker. With this kind of bargaining power, it doesn't make much difference what your competitors are charging. You can name your price, because you're the one they have to have.

If you can transform yourself from a qualified candidate into the candidate, you won't have much need for fancy negotiating tactics when it comes time to agree on terms. Get yourself in this position, and you can probably upgrade your job title. The company may entrust you with a wider range of responsibilities—which means richer experiences and more opportunities. You may be able to report to a higher-level supervisor and have greater decision-making power. All this translates to a higher salary, access to more privileges, and speedier career development.

If, on the other hand, the employer sees you as no more qualified or desirable than any of the other candidates, your efforts to significantly improve a job offer will almost certainly inspire a second look at your competitors. Making the company feel like it needs you, specifically, will get you a better deal than deploying every negotiating trick in the book from a position of weakness.

2. Your bargaining power reflects the company's experiences with you.

Bargaining power is the sum of all the impressions you've made. A referral from a respected source is a great first deposit in your power bank. More than one adds to your account. Enthusiastic references contribute still more. An impressive first interview, in which you articulate your strengths, show that

you know what it takes to do the job, and share some insights based on your own research, can be a big power boost.

If your follow-up to that first meeting demonstrates more work on your part, you get a second interview and more power. When your meetings with your potential colleagues go well, you raise your stock a bit more. Perhaps you can tackle a short-term assignment (for pay, if there is substantial work involved), and show off your talents. Now they really want you!

By the time you are in what's generally recognized as the negotiation process, you're dealing from a position of maximum strength.

3. The earlier you enter the hiring process, the more influence you have.

A company rarely decides to seek out a new employee on the spur of the moment. Unless it's simply a matter of replacing an employee who's moved on, such decisions typically follow a three-stage process:

Stage 1: A problem or need is identified. There's too much work to be done by the existing staff, a problem with quality or customer satisfaction, or a need to develop new business.

Stage 2: Solutions are considered. Should several employees' jobs be redefined so that their talents are put to better use? Should an existing staff member be moved to a new position? (If so, that person's old position will have to be filled.) Should a new employee be hired to fill the position? Or should most of the work be outsourced?

Stage 3: The job is defined. The company decides to create a new position. The next questions are: Where will the money come from? Who will the person report to? What will the job description include?

Only after all three stages are completed does the company go to the market—advertise the position, post it on the Internet, hire a recruiter to find the right person. If you enter the game at this stage, you're likely to face a fair amount of competition, which means diminished bargaining power. If you can enter at an earlier stage, you gain several advantages:

- You can influence how the company sees its needs and how best to address them. This is an opportunity to tailor the job description to fit your qualifications and make full use of your talents. It's also a chance to boost the job to the highest level possible—and more responsibility equals more money.

- You allow the company to solve the problem quickly, avoiding the time and expense of working through all three stages, not to mention sorting through hordes of applicants.

- Because at this point there are few—or no—other candidates, the company is less likely to base its compensation offer on what similarly qualified candidates might cost. And even if you can't get the salary as high as you'd like, you'll be in a prime position to win other forms of compensation and benefits.

Getting considered early usually means entering the discussions informally. If your first contact with the company is through an informational meeting (perhaps set up through one of your networking sources), you can talk about your background and interests without the pressure of an interview situation, get feedback on any research you've done, and learn about the industry and the business from an insider.

In the process, you may see a need or problem at the company that has not yet been defined (entering at stage one), or find out about one whose solution has not yet been settled (entering at stage two). You'll be able to follow up on the information meeting with a letter or e-mail describing the additional thinking or research you've done (based on the insider perspective you've gained), which sets you up for another meeting. Once you're in the discussion loop and have

established your credibility, you're in a prime position to land a position that's tailored for you. (*Job Hunting A to Z: The WetFeet Insider Guide to Landing the Job You Want* provides detailed advice on presenting yourself effectively and conducting informational meetings that lead to job opportunities.)

4. Taking on a short-term project can dramatically improve your bargaining power.

While you're holding informal discussions about the company's needs, you're in an excellent position to suggest that you take on a short-term project addressing a critical issue. (This is also a great way to make yourself stand out if you've entered the hiring process after stage three.) Possible projects include:

- Conducting a customer survey
- Organizing and running a focus group
- Evaluating a proposed employee-benefit program
- Exploring and reporting on better sources for contract manufacturing
- Flow-charting operating procedures and designing a new workflow
- Investigating the willingness of another organization (a complementary business or a nonprofit agency) to enter into an alliance
- Finding new business prospects

Properly structured, such a project gives you several potential advantages:

- You can demonstrate the quality of work, rather than relying solely on your resume and the inferences people make when interviewing you. Of course, it's essential that the demonstration show you in your best light—that you meet the deadline, produce more than you promise, and provide facts and insights that are clearly worth having. Spend whatever time it takes to make sure this is the outcome. (Don't take on a short-term project if you're not sure you can do a good job—shoddy work will make you look worse than if you'd done nothing at all.)

- You get to operate on the inside, where you'll get a full picture of the firm's needs. This kind of knowledge will prove valuable later when you're discussing the job and what you bring to it.

- You can charge a daily rate that may be substantially more than what you'd earn doing similar work as a full-time employee. So when the company does offer to bring you aboard, your frame of reference on salary—and theirs—is this daily rate, rather than the lower rate that might otherwise apply. For example, a short-term project rate of $450 a day translates, at 250 working days per year, to an annual salary of $112,500. All right, you may agree to a bargain rate of $95,000, considering that they're offering you a benefits package. Still, this is much better than the $70,000 you had previously hoped to get!

Note: Your daily rate depends on the nature of the assignment. If you're filling in for someone and need considerable supervision, the rate could reasonably be from 100 to 150 percent of that person's salary prorated by the day. (Go ahead and ask if you don't know what the person's salary is.) But if you're working on a high-priority project, adding your own expertise to the manager's, or improving business opportunities, for example, your rate can be considerably higher—as much as double a staff person's regular pay.

5. Know the market and develop alternative job offers.

Researching industry standards for compensation will help you advance your case. If you know what others are paying, you can use this information if the company seems to be giving you a lowball offer. This way you can express surprise—tactfully—at the proposed salary and have the figures to back up your reaction.

Even better is developing alternative job offers or hot prospects. You may well find something better, and the process will bolster your confidence and give the impression that you're a person in demand. People wait hours to eat at popular restaurants while less-celebrated spots, perhaps equally good, always have empty

tables. The same dynamics apply here. If a competitor thinks well enough of you to make an offer, the company you've set your sights on will probably make an extra effort to snag you.

We know what you're thinking, but inventing alternatives is no substitute for developing real ones. Real alternatives have the ring of truth and allow you to cite specific attractions as bargaining chips. Imaginary alternatives tend to sound phony, and you run the risk that the hiring manager will invite you to take the nonexistent offer. Then you'll have to scramble to find a plausible reason for taking the real job after all, which makes your bargaining position mighty weak.

Knowing that you have real alternatives will also help you ask for what you want with more firmness. You'll be able to walk away from the negotiation without anxiety rather than accept unsatisfactory terms. After all, there's little point in accepting an offer inferior to one you already have—or expect to have—in hand.

6. Establish your priorities, and evaluate offers accordingly.

Salary usually isn't the only consideration when evaluating a job offer. Other factors that may be important to you include:

- The quality of the learning opportunity
- Rapport with your supervisor
- Respect for your colleagues
- The workplace atmosphere, whether intense or relaxed, competitive or mutually supportive, chaotic or organized
- Other forms of compensation, such as bonuses or commission
- Benefits such as health insurance
- Perks and recognition (international travel and speaking opportunities, respectively)

- The company's prestige

- The importance or value of what the organization produces

- Career-advancement opportunities

- Vacation and time-off policies

- Flexibility of the work schedule

- Location

- Commuting distance and related considerations (availability of public transportation or parking)

- On-site facilities, such as fitness and child-care centers

One way to get a clear picture of how competing offers compare—or how a single offer compares with your dream job—is to create a decision matrix (see the Sample Decision Matrix on the next page). List the factors that matter most to you, then assign each a relative weight out of a total weight of 100 (e.g., career opportunity, 30; salary, 30; rapport with supervisor, 20; benefits, 10; location, 10). When you receive an offer, rate how strong the offer is on each factor, on a scale of zero to ten. Then multiply the weight for each factor by the rating you gave the company's offer on that factor. For example, if you gave salary a relative weight of 25 and rated Company X's salary offer at six, Company X would receive 150 points for salary. Add up the results for each factor, and you'll have a score for the offer out of a possible 1,000 points. Generally, you should not have to settle for an offer that scores less than 700 points. This exercise will help you to stay focused on the factors that are most important to you, identify your main negotiating points, and recognize when you should probably look elsewhere.

Sample Decision Matrix

Factor	Weight (Relative to 100%)	Offer's Rating (on a 0–10 scale)		
		Job A	Job B	Job C
Essential	(75%)			
Growth Opportunities	25	6 (=150)	9 (=225)	8 (=200)
Great Colleagues	15	7 (=105)	8 (=120)	6 (=90)
Challenging Work	15	5 (=75)	10 (=150)	8 (=120)
Travel Opportunities	10	3 (=30)	7 (=70)	9 (=90)
Compensation	10	9 (=90)	5 (=50)	7 (=70)
Nice to Have	(25%)			
Reasonable Hours	9	7 (=63)	3 (=27)	4 (=36)
Rapport with Supervisor	9	9 (=81)	5 (=45)	8 (=72)
Recognition	5	8 (=40)	4 (=20)	6 (=30)
Medical Benefits	2	2 (=4)	0 (=0)	2 (=4)
Total	100%	638	707	712

The Sample Decision Matrix above shows how one job seeker weighted her own preferences, giving each a percentage. She looked at three job offers and ranked the preferences on a zero-to-ten scale for each job. Job C had the highest overall score, but Job B was a close second. In fact, Job B might be the better choice because it scored higher in the "Essential" category.

7. Be aware of what the employer can offer.

The forms of potential compensation are many. Some of the following confer other benefits, but they all boil down to money:

- Salary (usually the base for figuring bonuses and raises)
- Signing bonus (often given if you are being induced to leave a good job)
- Moving allowance
- Bonuses (best if tied to measurable criteria)
- Early review for salary increase or promotion
- Commissions
- Health plan, and the company's share of the premium
- Tuition reimbursement
- Stock award or options
- 401(k) plan
- Severance package

Learn as much as you can about industry and company standards for each form of compensation before you sit down to negotiate. You'll find advice on when and how to negotiate for these and other items in "What's Negotiable?"

8. Assess your power position realistically.

If you've done a good job of building your perceived value and uniqueness and have convinced the employer of the need to sign you up right away, the initial offer may be much better than what the employer—or you—originally had in mind. And you may be able to make the offer even juicier by using some of the tactics described in the section of the same name.

But just as you shouldn't underestimate your bargaining power (you don't want to shortchange yourself), it's important not to overestimate it. To overestimate is to court resentment and lead the employer to search for someone less troublesome. Your tactics throughout the hiring process should reflect, as accurately as you can assess it, your actual bargaining power.

Some situations are inherently strong. Others have built-in weaknesses. (The Bargaining Power chart compares the two.) Also, your bargaining power may shift during the course of your interactions with the employer. Another good candidate enters the picture; your bargaining power declines. The employer's need to fill the position grows more urgent; your power increases. The company decides it needs someone with more experience than you to jump in at full speed; your power drops again. You perform admirably on a short-term project; your power grows. You flub it—sorry, your power vanishes. When the situation changes, you'll need to adjust your tactics accordingly.

If someone recommended you for the position or there's a recruiter involved, he or she may be able to tell you what's going on. But you need to learn to read the cues. Frequent calls, requests for references, and hopeful inquiries about your interest are all good signs. Phone calls unreturned for days, interviews repeatedly rescheduled, and vague put-offs don't bode well.

To avoid getting to this point, try to resolve any likely reasons for doubt early on. A less-than-glowing reference is better explained before the reference is checked than after. If an objection is raised by someone on the hiring team (too little employment continuity, the wrong kind of background), it's better to bring it up and discuss it, rather than let it eat away at your bargaining power.

9. Never be the first to name a salary.

If you name a figure in response to a question about your salary expectations, it could be well above what the employer had in mind, and your interviewer's thoughts will shift to another candidate. If the figure is too low, you'll be stuck with less than what the employer was planning to pay—and you may even come off as suddenly less qualified to boot. There is no need to fall into such a trap. The employer knows the responsibilities of the job better than you do, and so is better qualified to give it a dollar value. Once that happens, you are in an excellent position to discuss why you could bring more to the position someone else might.

10. Always negotiate with the decision maker.

You've just negotiated an excellent price on a new car and are ready to sign on the dotted line. Then the salesman tells you he has to clear everything with the boss. The boss (who remains faceless) sends word that he can't possibly go that low—his invoice price is just $100 less, not counting transportation charges. The salesman made a mistake. But he could do the deal for another $450, just to cover the transportation cost. He'll pay for your first oil change. What can you do? You've burned up most of your Sunday already, and you want to drive home in that sports car!

A word to the wise: Don't deal with intermediaries in your job negotiations, lest you end up in a similar situation. Intermediaries—human resources representatives, staffing specialists, recruiters, or occasionally someone dele-gated by the hiring manager—usually don't know as much about the job as the person you'll actually be working for, nor do they have the same concern about losing you if the negotiations go astray. They have a lot less latitude to take special circumstances into account. And they're often unaware of what can be done

"creatively"—flexible working hours, extra vacation days, a signing bonus, or company-furnished laptop—to sweeten the pot.

11. Try to create situations that benefit you and the company.

Listen closely to what the hiring manager says and find out what his or her most pressing needs are. If you can meet some or all of those needs, the manager can probably meet yours. Suggest solutions that are mutually beneficial, that are less costly for the firm, or that let you meet each other halfway.

Finally, avoid pushing things so far that your deal will be resented. You may become the victim of over-eager scrutiny, be criticized unfairly, or otherwise find yourself made to be uncomfortable. You have to live in the climate you create.

📁 Bargaining Power

Stronger	Weaker
You were strongly recommended.	You came in through a job posting.
You enter the picture when there are few or no other candidates.	You enter the picture when there are many candidates
You have lots of relevant experience and accomplishments.	You have limited relevant experience or accomplishments.
Your discussions focus on the job.	Your discussions focus primarily on your qualifications.
You've done a good job of building your perceived value.	You've left it to the employer to assess your value.
The employer is concerned about your taking a job elsewhere.	The employer is unconcerned about your going elsewhere.
The hiring manager checks in with you frequently and answers your calls quickly.	Your phone never rings, and your calls are taken by an assistant.
They call to make sure you received the offer letter—and that you like it.	There's little or no follow-up on the offer letter.
They are courting you and give special attention to your feelings about the company.	There's no courting or concern for your feelings about the company.
They mention attractive extras such as a good signing bonus, stock options, and a generous moving allowance.	They seem to have a take-it-or-leave-it attitude.
You have attractive alternatives and are not worried about your prospects.	You're feeling desperate and afraid of losing this opportunity.

Note: You should make some allowances if the hiring manager appears to be dealing with urgent business or is just disorganized and inefficient. Don't give up too easily! Constructive persistence—not nagging—can pay off.

Strategic Negotiation

- Strategic Negotiation Fundamentals

- Know the Market

- Discussing Your Salary History

- What's Negotiable?

Strategic Negotiation Fundamentals

Strategic negotiation aims for more than simply landing the job—it's the conscious process of creating conditions that will give you that job on the best possible terms. You're working toward three objectives concurrently: 1) improving your chances of getting the job offer; 2) increasing the value the employer places on the position; and 3) creating the perception that you are the person for the job.

Think of your strategy as being built on four cornerstones, each of which will lift you to a higher and more solid starting point for discussions on salary and benefits than you would otherwise have. Let's examine them one at a time.

Self-Knowledge and Effective Presentation

How can you expect a potential employer to understand your strengths, goals, and working style if you're not clear about them yourself?

Your resume is but a scanty summary of who you are. Take the trouble to list some of your proudest accomplishments, then write a short "story" about each of them, following a situation-action-result pattern. Try to find common threads in these stories that reflect your major strengths. These might be creative problem-solving, skill at organizing facts, the ability to listen well and find a consensus, talent for motivating others, thinking well under pressure, or whatever. These become the main theme of your presentation: what you've accomplished, how you accomplished it, and how you can put these strengths to work in a new position.

Think about your work habits as well. Do you work best in a high-pressure atmosphere or one that's more relaxed? Do you like to work alone or as part of a group? Or do you prefer a combination of the two? Do you like a lot of socializing or prefer to be more private? These factors will affect your happiness and performance at a new job, so you should consider them when making a job decision.

Ask other people about their impressions of you, particularly people you plan to use as references. Their responses will help you select what to emphasize in the messages you convey about yourself.

Develop a two-minute presentation on yourself, and use it whenever possible. Devote about 30 seconds to your career, your educational background, and your key strengths; 60 seconds to describing two key accomplishments that illustrate those strengths (the stories will come in handy here); and the final 30 seconds to the kind of work and responsibilities you're seeking. Don't let yourself go over two-and-a-half minutes, lest you sound too self-centered, or under one-and-a-half minutes, lest you seem lightweight. Practice delivering this presentation, not as a word-for-word recital, but extemporaneously, based on the key points you want to make. (You'll find more on constructing and delivering presentations in *Job Hunting A to Z: The WetFeet Insider Guide to Landing the Job You Want.*)

Use this two-minute presentation at the beginning of every information meeting and first interview. It will give you immediate credibility and answer most of the interviewer's questions about your background and goals, leaving you free to ask questions about the company and the job. Be prepared with great questions, and you'll enhance the good first impression.

How the Employer Values the Job

Often a position that seems mundane is vitally important to the business. Performing it well can bring in extra revenue or stop major losses. Doing mediocre work can be costly. Your first questions should draw the interviewer out about the nature of the job. Your next goal is to make sure the interviewer recognizes the job's full value. You can do this by identifying a challenge the position presents and taking the interviewer through a series of questions evaluating that challenge. The two sample dialogues that follow illustrate this process.

Valuing the Work: Home-Care Situation

You: I understand you want me to stay with Mr. Lasher between 8 p.m. and midnight Saturday evening?

Client: Yes, that's right. The pay would be ten dollars per hour, assuming you make your own transportation arrangements.

You: I have a car, so transportation's not a problem. What I'm wondering is if you have any special concerns about Mr. Lasher.

Client: Well, one of the problems caused by his Parkinson's disease is that he needs assistance getting around—but he won't necessarily tell you that.

You: I have read up on Parkinson's disease, so I'm familiar with many of the issues. Does Mr. Lasher have any other conditions that might require emergency attention?

Client: He had heart-bypass surgery a year-and-a-half ago, but no recent difficulties. I'm concerned, but less so than right after the surgery.

You: Still, I'm glad to be aware of this. Could you leave his Medicare card where I can find it, and can I call for medical assistance if necessary?

Client: Certainly. I want him to have the best of medical attention, if it's needed—which, of course, I hope it won't be.

You: It sounds as though my job on Saturday night is to provide Mr. Lasher with friendly attention, help him manage whatever normal tasks might be required, be on the alert for anything unusual, and to take responsibility for his well-being if there's an emergency. Is that essentially right?

Client: Yes! It sounds like you're well-prepared to take care of my father-in-law.

You: I'll be glad to do it, but my rate—reasonable I think, given the responsibility—is $60 for the evening up to 12 o'clock.

Client: That's more than I expected to pay, but you seem like someone I can trust, so I'll agree to that.

Valuing the Work: Inventory-Management Situation

You: From our discussion last time, I understand the position you have in mind for me is inventory management. Could you tell more about what your needs in that area might be? (Actually, you've spent the time since the last meeting learning all you could about the subject.)

Employer: Yes. We need someone to keep track of our daily incoming shipments, our daily outgoing shipments, and our inventory levels. That sort of thing.

You: Are you experiencing a problem now—revenues not in synch with other numbers, or other discrepancies? (An on-target question based on thinking about what inventory management involves.)

Employer: Unfortunately, yes. We have a shrinkage rate of about 2 percent, which is way too high. And too many damaged goods, which costs us plenty.

You: You told me earlier that monthly sales are about $600,000, so if I'm right, you're losing $12,000 a month in shrinkage. And about how much would you say the damaged-goods problem is causing?

Employer: At least that much—maybe more.

You: If you had a system for relating orders to shipments, outbound quality assurance, and damage accountability, would that help you with your customers relations, too? (A shrewd question, based on an article you read in *Industry Week* about a company's new inventory management system.)

Employer: Definitely. Too often the wrong materials go to a job site, or some have to be returned, and it takes time and patience to get it straightened out.

You: And there's a the risk the customer will go elsewhere in the future, right? What would it cost you to replace a major account? (This shows that you know how to relate improved practices to tangible value.)

Employer: A lot. It's taken years to build up our 15 major accounts.

You: If I can develop a system that reduces shrinkage to a negligible level, and cuts shipment errors by 75 percent or more, wouldn't that be pretty valuable to you? (Audacious, but you aren't saying you can do it alone, or in a month.)

Employer: Definitely! I'd be happy to get you a bonus if you could do that.

You: I've met some big challenges before, but I'll need your cooperation to do this. And I'd be glad to discuss a bonus, but I'll also need a higher base salary than what you mentioned.

Employer: Well—let's talk about it. What do you have in mind?

The candidate seems to think pretty quickly here, which creates more credibility. But if this is your second meeting with the manager, you've had time to do some thinking, research, and planning, and to come up with questions that lead the discussion where you want it to go.

In both cases the job seeker guides the discussion by asking questions. The job seeker may have known or have been able to guess the answers to some of these questions, but by having the interviewer state the case, you strengthen his or her commitment to that interpretation.

Also note that in both situations the questions follow a sequence. First are questions that characterize the situation: Mr. Lasher needs help getting around, and careful attention. Inventories are out of control. Next come questions that elicit the reasons for the situation: Mr. Lasher has Parkinson's disease and has had heart surgery. There is no set system for ensuring that shipments match orders. The following questions attempt to increase the perceived urgency or importance of solving the problem: Mr. Lasher could experience a medical emergency. The company may lose customers to another vendor. The final questions confirm the value of a solution to the employer: Peace of mind. Satisfied, loyal customers.

Using this simple construction, you can nudge future employers into upping—in their minds and their own words—the value of the position.

It takes some practice to develop such questions well and use them skillfully. As with other negotiating strategies and tactics, we suggest you perfect this technique in situations with less at stake than a job negotiation—renting an apartment, say, or negotiating group rates for a weekend trip with friends.

How the Employer Values You in the Job

It's not enough that the hiring manager realizes the value of the job. He or she must also see you as the best person to do the job. You have a big head start, of course, if you've created a sense of urgency about filling the position and gained acknowledgment of its value. You now seem insightful and knowledgeable.

But performance is still paramount in the employer's mind. Can you do the job? Will you be motivated to do the job, persist in the face of obstacles, and meet deadlines while doing quality work? Will you fit in well with the company's culture, needs, and expectations?

To answer the "Can you do it?" question, the employer usually considers your resume, your responses to interview questions, and your references, and compares all candidates in those areas. But you can do more to distinguish yourself from the pack.

One option is a testimonial letter describing how you solved a problem or came through in a crisis. For maximum credibility, the letter should be addressed to you, not "to whom it may concern," and phrased as an expression of appreciation for a job well done. If you don't have a letter like this on hand, you can ask one of your references to write one—you might even get faster results by providing a draft.

You may be able to demonstrate your abilities by taking on a short-term project as described in "Building Your Bargaining Power" or auditioning, by briefly performing some aspect for the job—customer service, teaching, programming, or selling, for example.

Yet another way of addressing the "Can you do it?" question is to prepare a concept paper like the one designed to address weak qualifications, but focused on the necessary skills for doing the job well. The paper should identify each

skill and show that you possess it. It needn't be long, although it may run more than a page if complex issues are involved. This kind of presentation helps the employer envision you in the job. Do more than other candidates to demonstrate your abilities, and you'll add to your bargaining power.

The employer's chief concerns are:

- Will you meet deadlines?
- Will you be challenged and interested in this position?
- Will you stay committed or hit the road the minute a slightly better offer comes along?

To address these concerns, you first need to ask yourself some questions—and answer them honestly. Is this a job you care about enough to do what it takes to meet expectations? If you do meet expectations, will the money, recognition, or intrinsic value of the work be rewarding enough to you? Can the expectations be met? If you think the manager's expectations are unrealistic, but the job appeals to you otherwise, try listing the main responsibilities as you understand them and breaking each one down into its component parts. Tell the manager you want to review the list and make sure you're correctly estimating the time needed to do the job at the level expected. The manager may classify some duties as less important or point out where help is available. You can then add up the time needed for each task, plus meetings and administrative work, and get a clear idea about whether the job can be done in the hours you're willing to devote to it.

Think about whether you'll be happy in the job six months from now. Will there be enough challenges and learning opportunities to keep the job fresh over time? Is solving the initial problem what intrigues you, rather than the ongoing responsibilities? Now is the time to recognize the situation for what it is. Do you commonly fall prey to the grass-is-always-greener syndrome, or do

you usually stick with what you start? If you tend to jump from task to task, maybe consulting or a start-up would suit you better than a more structured environment. Only when you are clear on your preferences and feelings about the job can you make the kind of compelling, from-the-heart pitches likely to win over an astute manager.

Next, consider the homily, "Actions speak louder than words." When the employer is on the verge of making an offer, but you haven't yet discussed pay and benefits, look for a way to make an investment in the job. You could give the employer a list of things you'd try to achieve in the first 30 days, noting the actions you'd take to meet these goals. Maybe you could accomplish a few of these beforehand. If so, they will serve as handy illustrations of your willingness to do this job when you sit down to discuss pay and benefits.

Finally, think about how you'll fit into the company's culture, needs, and expectations. Because even if you get top marks for performance and motivation, the employer will be thinking, "Can we live with you while you do the job?" Ask yourself the following questions, and consider how well your answers match what your potential colleagues' practices seem to be.

- Do you like to speak your mind and expect others to do the same? Or do you think direct confrontation gets in the way of good team functioning?

- Do you like to establish your own record and be recognized for it, or do you think expectations and credit should be focused more on the team?

- How do you deal with conflict?

If you're convinced you'll fit right in, the next step is to convince the employer. Find a way to slip comments on your work style into your discussions. Try using a lead-in phrase such as: "You may be wondering whether I have the calmness under pressure to maintain a productive, team-oriented approach." Then go on to illustrate by describing a situation that shows you at your best.

The upshot is that you can make a big difference in how potential employers envision you in the job you're seeking by providing positive—and convincing—answers to the employer's three fundamental questions:

- Do you have the skills and experience to do the job?
- Will you do the job? Are you motivated, persistent, and responsible enough?
- Will you get along with your colleagues and fit in with the company's culture?

Now that you've added substantially to your perceived value and bargaining power, you should be a top candidate. At this point you need to think about how to set up the discussion of salary and benefits to your best advantage.

Sample Concept Paper

Skill Required	How I've Demonstrated this Skill
Ability to recruit, train, and retain a well-qualified and motivated staff	Seven years of successful staff recruitment and training at British Airways, with several citations for excellence
Ability to form and maintain positive relationships with engineering, manufacturing, field service, and other departments	Interfaced positively with angry union representatives, upset passengers, anxious middle managers, and harried airport representatives; promoted partly because of skill in resolving conflicts
Ability to provide proactive rather than reactive service that will result in bottom-line payoffs from losses to high profits	Helped create the highly successful "Putting People First" program, which raised customer ratings of British Airways dramatically and contributed to BA's turnaround
Setting high standards, enforcing them, and living by them	Instituted service standards and tracking measures and achieved sustained improvement on each measure
Flexible approach recognizing differing customer needs, product types, stages in product life cycles	Managed counter services, baggage handling, ramp services, boarding and gates, and cabin crew training at various times, performing through storms, strikes, slowdowns, and other adverse circumstances

I hope you will see my experience and accomplishments as relevant and valuable in the position of customer service manager at Axlon Logistics Services. I am confident and enthusiastic about what can be accomplished!

Sincerely,

Patricia Dillingham

Know the Market

One of the key principles of strategic negotiation is to know the market. For maximum leverage, you need to answer the following questions:

- What is the going rate for the position? (This will probably require some research—likely sources include industry trade magazines, websites, and Sibson and Mercer or other salary surveys used by human resources departments.)

- What positives or negatives apply—to you or the job—that might justify a deviation from the going rate?

- How much bargaining power do you really have? (See the Bargaining Power chart.)

- What factors are most important to you, and which of them might be negotiable? (Consult your decision matrix.)

- What is your best alternative prospect if the negotiations don't work out?

- What is the lowest salary you can accept?

Another key principle that comes into play here is to never be the first to name a salary. If you ask for too much, you risk scaring away the employer; if you ask for too little, you shortchange yourself. Of course, many employers will try to pin you down on this near the beginning of the interviewing process to save themselves from considering candidates who are out of range. This seems reasonable enough, until you consider that the employer's view of reasonable compensation for you is subject to change—for the better, if you build up cornerstones one, two, and three. You need to buy time to put your strategies into action. Which means you'll have to prepare yourself to resist requests to name your price.

It's okay to be open about what you've earned in the past. Answering honestly any questions about your salary history is a good approach—it makes you seem open, and they could get the information on their own anyway. You should put some distance, though, between what you have earned and the current situation.

Discussing Your Salary History

Say you're interviewing for a corporate training position that you think should pay $60,000 to $80,000, but your last job as a Berlitz instructor paid only $40,000. Here's how you might handle the discussion:

Employer: Could you tell me what you were earning at Berlitz?

You: Yes. I accepted a position at only $40,000 because I wanted to develop complete fluency in Spanish, and the schedule allowed me to continue with my human resources program at Whittier College. I'm sure my language ability would be valuable here.

Employer: What would you expect to be earning here at Veratron in this position?

You: I'm sure you've considered what the job involves and will offer a fair salary. I'm relying on that.

Employer: Don't you have a minimum figure in mind?

You: I have several opportunities I'm considering, and each has different characteristics. I have to take all the circumstances into account. Maybe you could give some idea of the range for this position?

Employer: Well, let's leave that for later, assuming we decide there's a good fit. Okay?

You: Fine. Let's do that. (You are now free to use some of your value-increasing strategies.)

Or the dialogue might take this turn:

Employer: The range is $50,000 to $70,000, depending on experience.

You: Hmm. I'd consider something in the neighborhood of $70,000 or maybe a bit more. (Again, you are now free to use some of your value-increasing strategies.)

Finally, recall another key principle: Make sure you negotiate with the decision maker, not an intermediary. The decision maker—usually the hiring manager, but sometimes a recruiter—has a far better understanding of the job than an intermediary such as a human resources manager. The decision maker also has a greater sense of urgency about filling the position, and more flexibility in addressing your needs. Besides, this is the person you'll be working with—you want to make sure you reach a mutually satisfying agreement.

Strategic Negotiation

Good

"My goal is to join a quality company where I can make a contribution and learn, so the starting salary is less important to me than the opportunity. Can we talk more about what the job would entail?" (You refocus the conversation on the nature of the job.)

"I've looked at salary surveys, and frankly, they're more confusing than helpful because of the differences among the companies in this field—quality, size, location. Perhaps you could tell me how your company values this position." (You paint a picture of yourself as someone who does research and is thoughtful about it, while leading the interviewer to give you information.)

"At this point, I'm most interested in finding a job that lets me use and develop my skills. I'm really excited about your company, and I'm willing to consider any competitive offer." (Also focuses on the job, and confirms your interest in the company without undermining your position.)

"I'm willing to consider reasonable offers." (An obvious brush-off, but the interviewer might let it go.)

Bad

"I haven't really had a chance to give it much thought." (Perhaps you don't give much thought to other important matters, either.)

"As much as you can afford to pay me!" (Okay, this could be funny with the right delivery—if the interviewer has a sense of humor. But even then it's not an effective put-off: The likely response after ha, ha, ha? "Seriously, though . . . ")

"At least $60,000." (The most you'll get is $60,000, even if $65,000 was budgeted. See how naming a figure undercuts your ability to negotiate?)

"I'm expensive, but worth it." (Misguided attempt at humor; sounds clichéd and conceited.)

Note: If the interviewer is so determined to nail you on your salary expectations that you can't proceed with the interview until you name a figure, give a range with a low end that's just above what you think the company's high end will be or better, what the person tells you it is, if you can get that far). That way, the low end of your range and the top end of theirs will be relatively close, you still have some basis for negotiation, and the interview can proceed.

But what if it's the HR manager who sends you the offer letter or asks what you would accept? Try the following approach:

You: Thank you for your offer letter. I wanted to let you know that I received it, but I have quite a few meetings scheduled over the next several days, so it's going to be several days before I can give the offer proper attention.

HR: (Concerned because of your reference to all those meetings) Well, can you tell me what your initial reaction is?

You: I still have a few questions about the job's responsibilities and Ron's [the hiring manager's] expectations of me. I'd like to set up another meeting with him to go over those—and also I'd appreciate the opportunity to meet Charlene Osgood [Ron's boss]. (You're now positioned to negotiate with Charlene as well, in case she turns out to be an obstacle and the final decision maker.)

HR: Fine. I'll ask Ron to get you on his calendar today or tomorrow, if possible. I'll leave it to him to make arrangements with Charlene. When are you available? (He passes along his perceptions to Ron and asks Ron to meet with you.)

Your discussion with the hiring manager should begin with your stated agenda—a review of responsibilities and expectations. This will give you the opportunity to reinforce his or her sense of your value. Now you can discuss the offer.

What's Negotiable?

Generally, what's negotiable in a compensation package depends on two key factors. The first is the bargaining power you've built up—by virtue of your successful demonstration of your abilities, the employer's perception of the value of the position and sense of urgency about filling it, and how the negotiations are set up. Most of these factors are somewhat subjective—they depend largely on the hiring manager's mind-set and what you've been able to do to influence it.

The other factor is objective constraints. These are barriers that can't easily be moved no matter what the hiring manager thinks. Such constraints might include:

- Union contract terms. If you are signing on as a teacher in a unionized school district, for example, your pay will be predetermined. (But you might be able to negotiate your school assignment, the grade level you teach, and any extra duties.)

- Policies set by the board of directors, such as a formula for determining pay. (But such policies often have loopholes that you can slip through if you have enough bargaining power.)

- Policies set by management, such as not providing allowances. (But you may be able to substitute a different benefit to compensate.)

- Group-hire situations, such as internships, where everyone is paid the same standard salary. (But kickers such as a moving allowance, low-interest loans, tuition reimbursement, time off for pursuing advanced education, and other accommodations may be made for must-have candidates.)

- The pay level of your peers or the person you would report to. This is often a constraint because the manager fears your colleagues will be dissatisfied if you get paid more than they do. (But with creative negotiation you can win

other forms of compensation and valuable benefits, without setting yourself up for peer-group resentment.)

As you can see, even with objective constraints, there's often more room for negotiation than you are initially led to believe—if the employer really wants you. To maximize your chances of overcoming barriers, try to suggest a situation that's a winner for the manager, too, such as:

- "If I attend night school to learn more about operational simulation, could I be of greater value to you, and maybe justify tuition reimbursement?"

- "I know that the school needs to attract students as well as teachers. Could I do some marketing work in addition to teaching? Would that help you meet my salary needs?"

- "Would it be easier for you to use me on a consulting basis, until you're sure I can handle the vendor relationships, and then we could come back to the salary issue?"

Still, there comes a time when the hiring manager can't go any further in meeting your needs. When you hear something like, "Please consider this our final offer," "I just can't go beyond what I've agreed to already," or "I think your expectations are beyond what we can do," continued pushing will only cause alienation and most likely a negative outcome for you. Better to recognize this and end the discussion politely by saying either "Thank you very much. I appreciate your efforts to meet my needs, and you can be sure I'll do my best to meet your expectations" (if you are accepting the offer) or "Thank you very much. I appreciate your efforts to meet my needs, and I'll give your offer careful thought" (if you're not ready to accept it).

Note: If you do succeed in cutting a special deal that might be the envy of your peers, be discreet about it. You won't score any points by causing unhappiness in your work group and making your manager regret trying to accommodate you.

Responsibilities and Opportunities

The starting place for thinking about negotiations should be job responsibilities and opportunities, not compensation. This is true for several reasons:

- Discussion of responsibilities and opportunities is what gives you access to the decision maker rather than an intermediary.

- Your responsibilities and opportunities will be the most important factor in your job satisfaction—much more than your compensation, if you're paid at all fairly. By clarifying these responsibilities, you'll be able to make a better assessment of whether the position is right for you and to suggest modifications that might make it more appealing.

- There's a good chance you and the employer will find that you can make a greater contribution than originally supposed, which may mean better compensation.

Here's a sample discussion of responsibilities:

You: Thanks for taking the time to meet with me again. As I said, I'd like to review the responsibilities of the project coordinator.

Employer: Well, I'd want you to keep tabs on the various elements of the project, identifying any roadblocks and bringing them to my attention and tracking project expenses.

You: I can certainly do that. And I assume you'd like me to use project-planning and spreadsheet software and to make appropriate slides for management presentations?

(Accepts the job requirements, then makes suggestions for how to increase the value of the work.)

Employer: Yes, that would be very helpful. I wasn't sure how comfortable you were with those programs; they are a lot of help in managing a project.

You: Yes, they are. And I hope I can help people find ways to overcome roadblocks or delays, so you don't need be involved in issues that can be resolved at a lower level. How does that sound?

(Shows understanding of the value of the manager's time and indicates confidence and initiative.)

Employer: Great. Just give me a weekly write-up, and come see me if you need my input.

You: Well, I'll certainly do my best to get the project back on track. I know how important it is to the company. Can we review my performance in three months? I like to know that I'm delivering what's expected.

(Shows commitment and accountability—and sets the candidate up for a raise in three months.)

Employer: Of course, and I hope to be able to justify an increase at that time, if you do as well as I believe you might.

You: Thanks. One other thing: I may need to work late some evenings to make calls to Asia and start early to reach people in Israel. May I have some discretion in working from home occasionally, as long as I give you an accounting?

(Makes a reasonable request, putting it in the context of a benefit to the company rather than personal convenience.)

Employer: That shouldn't be a problem as long as we're in good communication and the job gets done.

You: It will. Thank you for discussing this with me.

Salary

We repeat: Let the employer name a salary, either verbally or in a written offer letter. Then you can negotiate. You are in a much stronger position to discuss salary if you've done some homework. To get internal data on salary ranges, you may need to tap your inside sources, such as people who interviewed you, people who referred you, or former employees if you know anyone. If you know the going rate inside and outside the company, you'll have good justification for requesting a higher salary if the offer falls below either level. Here is a sample dialogue:

Manager: We're impressed with what you have to offer, Betty, but we're not sure we can afford you. What are your salary expectations?

Betty: I need to take into account a number of factors, including the job responsibilities, the learning opportunity, and the working environment. So I'm not set on a specific figure. Can you tell me what you think would be fair and reasonable for what I bring to this position?

Manager: The position, as we've defined it, pays in the range of $50,000 to $70,000, depending on experience.

Betty: Hmm . . . $70,000 is somewhat below what I've found to be typical in the industry for a position of this responsibility, but I'm glad to hear that experience figures into the equation.

Manager: Well, there are limits to what I can do beyond the defined range, but I may be able to come up with a little more if I allow for your graphic-design skills. We may be able to save a little on what we're now spending on contract design work.

Betty: That sounds good. Thank you for offering to look at possibilities. Perhaps you can put your best offer into writing so I can give it serious thought.

(A written offer is harder to disavow than a verbal one.)

Signing Bonus

Employers often offer a signing bonus when they can't pay a competitive salary right away or when they're luring someone away from another firm. Because they're not part of the regular payroll, these bonuses are hidden from view—which allows a manager to keep to the departmental salary structure. A signing bonus can range from modest—$1,000 or so—to substantial, depending on how much the firm wants you.

Keep in mind that companies often delay payment of signing bonuses to prevent recipients from collecting the money and then taking off to another opportunity. A common pay-out schedule is half in six months and the balance in twelve months. If you're not satisfied with a company's bonus offer, you may be able to increase it by agreeing to have it payable over a year or two. This lets the employer push some of your payment into the next budget cycle or even the one beyond that. Just remember: You'll lose any unpaid balance if you choose to leave.

Moving Allowance

A moving allowance is an extra enticement, much like a signing bonus, and depending on the circumstances, you may qualify to receive it tax-free.

Some companies will reimburse you for nearly all moving expenses, including hired movers, temporary living quarters, and sometimes even costs associated with real-estate transactions. Others offer a fixed sum, which may or may not

cover all your expenses. The allowance you get is often negotiable, because it's a nonrecurring cost for the company.

Bonuses and Commissions

Most sales people receive a relatively modest salary, but earn a commission on sales or get bonuses for meeting specified goals. (Sometimes both bonuses and commissions apply). A company's commission and bonus structure may be fixed, but more often it's open to negotiation.

Factors you may want to negotiate include:

- Sales goals
- Your commission percentage, standards you must meet to earn it, and additional rewards for exceeding goals
- The size and location of your sales territory, degree of exclusivity, and access to specific accounts
- Length of time you'll be able to keep the territory or accounts if you meet your goals
- Requirements for earning a bonus

You don't have to work in sales to qualify for incentive pay. If the company has a commission or bonus program in place, you may be able to identify measurable goals—such as a bonus or commission tied to the success of a sales team you support—that would qualify you to participate. If the company doesn't have an incentive program, you may be able to design one that's specific to your job.

For example:

- A reward for completing a behind-schedule project on time
- A reward for recovering a business relationship that has gone sour
- A bonus based on measurable improvement in customer satisfaction
- A bonus based on money saved through operational streamlining

- A finder's fee for recruiting needed staff members
- A bonus or commission tied to the number of new customers brought in by marketing programs

The possibilities depend largely on your ability to come up with relevant measures of performance and to demonstrate the value to the business if you reach your goals. This is an area where creative thinking pays off.

Review Date

In most organizations, employees receive annual performance and salary reviews. Even if you haven't been promoted or assigned new responsibilities, you can expect a raise of some amount if your performance is up to standard and the organization is doing even modestly well. An exceptional year may mean bigger raises or one-time bonuses.

Once you've negotiated your salary, you may want to request an earlier-than-usual performance review. If you think you'll be able to demonstrate that you're contributing well beyond your job description, or better yet, to reach agreed-upon goals, you may want to request a review after six months—or even three, if you can make a substantial impact that soon.

The value to you can be considerable. Let's say 5 percent annual raises are the norm. A six-month review that nets you 5 percent puts you in line for a full-year review that will likely result in an additional 2.5 to 5 percent. This can boost your paycheck thousands of dollars over what you would have received without the early review, and yet, an early review is fairly easy for most managers to grant. After all, good managers prefer early productivity and accountability, especially with new hires.

Stock Options

Several years ago, when initial public offerings by companies like Yahoo, Netscape, and Amazon were turning twenty- and thirty-something employees into instant millionaires, everyone wanted to get a hold of stock options. Those go-go dot com days are over. Still, stock options can sometimes help sweeten the pot. They're most common and potentially lucrative at start-up and early-stage companies. Larger, established companies frequently have option programs; these tend to be less negotiable, offer relatively few shares, and are sometimes restricted to middle and upper management. Options in such cases will rarely make a major difference in your near-term wealth, though over ten to 15 years they may amount to a good chunk of money.

The number of options granted is more negotiable at early-stage companies. The key to increasing your allotment is demonstrating that a greater ownership position will be an incentive for you to deliver extraordinary value.

This is where those fifth-grade fraction lessons come in handy. There's only so much pie, and you can't expect to get a quarter of it in a manager's position. More likely, you'll be debating over 1,000 shares equal to 0.2 percent of the company versus 1,500 equal to 0.3 percent. Make sure you do the math—10,000 options may sound like a lot, but it makes a big difference whether there the total number of shares is one million or fifty million.

Other considerations: If you're signing on with a start-up, those options will be worth something only if and when the company is sold or goes public. And there's usually a long vesting period before you can exercise your options. So if you're planning on a short stay (or the company decides that's what you'll have), options will be just worthless paper. And, of course, do keep in mind that the vast majority of start-ups never takes off.

Tuition Reimbursement and Educational Opportunities

Wouldn't it be great if you could learn a career-advancing new skill or earn an advanced degree on your employer's dime—and even your employer's time? Well, you can.

Tuition reimbursement is a standard benefit that could be worth thousands of dollars. But don't get carried away with fantasies about afternoon art classes— you'll probably have to attend school at night, and you'll have to be learning something the employer believes will help you in your job and thus benefit the company. Be prepared to demonstrate how the courses you plan to take will increase your efficiency, generate ideas, or otherwise make you a more valuable employee. Some employers make loans rather than tuition grants, then forgive part of the loan for each year you remain an employee after concluding the education. Try to arrange for the balance of any loan to be forgiven if you are laid off.

Your employer may also sponsor educational opportunities ranging from informal, on-the-job learning and mentoring to formal programs involving regular courses and seminars. Eligibility for company-sponsored training can be a great perk, especially early in your career.

Recruiters say prospective hires can score major points by expressing an interest in continuing education—a benefit that may not cost much, but one that is good for both the company and the employee.

Profit-Sharing and 401(k) Programs

There are two forms of profit sharing. One is a form of incentive pay based on the company's performance. You and the company agree that a percentage of your compensation will be based on the firm's overall profits or profits from

Strategic Negotiation

certain deals. The other is pension profit sharing, in which the employer contributes a certain amount to your pension plan each year—usually figured as a percentage of your salary—based on the company's profitability.

A 401(k) plan lets you have the company set aside a portion of your pretax income (up to a legal limit) in a tax-deferred investment account. Most employers will also kick in full or partial matching contributions. In principle, the money is supposed to remain in the account until you retire, but certain plans let you borrow against it or make early withdrawals to cover expenses defined as critical, such as buying a home, paying your kids' college tuition, or medical care. Pension profit-sharing and 401(k) plans must conform to government regulations, so their terms are not negotiable. They are worth considering, though, when evaluating job alternatives.

Health Insurance

Company-sponsored health plans vary widely, and many smaller firms don't offer any form of medical insurance. The provisions of the plans won't be negotiable. Expect to pay at least part of the premium yourself (the days of free-ride insurance are over), and look for your employer to offer at least two options—a managed-care plan or HMO and a more traditional fee-for-service plan with a higher copayment.

While you can dip into your after-tax income to buy health insurance or join an HMO, it's obviously better to have your employer pay part of the premium and take your contribution from your pretax earnings. Before you decide to accept a job offer without health coverage, you should factor in the cost of purchasing insurance, unless you enroll in your spouse's company plan. You may be able to persuade the employer to reimburse you for the cost or pay you a higher salary to compensate for the lack of health coverage.

WetFeet®

Work Schedule

Your work schedule is usually decreed by the corporate norm, and you'll want to know what it is before you sign on. While nine-to-five jobs still exist, eight-to-six jobs are more common. What can you do if the normal schedule doesn't suit you? You may be able to negotiate a flexible schedule or permission to work at home one or two days a week. Just be aware that, in either case, your colleagues—and your manager—will be on the alert for any signs that you're slacking off, so make sure the work gets done. You may be better off proving yourself first and then negotiating a special schedule. If you find yourself working long hours that go beyond the corporate norm, you may be able to negotiate comp time—generally, an hour of time off for each hour of over-time. Many companies will even let you cash in unused comp time at the end of the year. Just make sure you have good documentation.

Vacation Time

Most U.S. companies determine paid vacation time by a formula based on how long you've been with the company—say, two weeks for the first three years, with an additional week tacked on at four years and another at ten. This may be negotiable, however, especially if most of people in your group are eligible for more than the minimum vacation, most people at your level are eligible for more, or you agree to take your time off at 15- to 20-week intervals, so your excess allotment isn't apparent. You may also be able to negotiate additional time off if you're willing to take it without pay.

Be cautious in this area, though: If you make vacation time the first item on your negotiating agenda, the employer might start to wonder about your enthusiasm with the job. It's best to address time off as more of an afterthought.

Severance Pay

Mergers, acquisitions, disappointing sales, natural disasters—all can lead to layoffs, and even stellar performers can find themselves ushered out the door. Newcomers usually get meager severance pay, so you may want to negotiate a commitment for a better send-off—say, three months' pay—if your employment is terminated through no fault of your own.

This should be the last thing you discuss in your negotiations. Termination is regarded in many circles as corporate death, and it's a subject many people would like to avoid. When you do bring it up, treat it as a conjecture: "What if the company were bought, and the new owner decided my job would be perfect for his unemployed nephew? What would I get in the way of severance pay?"

Finally, get the deal in writing—your manager may be laid off too!

Know Your Priorities

Your first thought after considering all these options may be "I want it all!" Ask for everything, though, and you may end up getting nothing. A long list of requests and demands—flextime, comp time, special bonuses, extra stock options, a higher-than-usual salary—looks like the sign of a high-maintenance employee, which could give the hiring manager cold feet.

You're better off concentrating on the two or three things that matter the most to you and considering other options only as part of your decision matrix for evaluating offers.

Tactics

- Obtaining the Offer

- Taking Stock

- Selecting Your Response

- The Employer's Bag of Tricks

- Mind Your Manners

- Negotiating No-Nos

Obtaining the Offer

You've built up your bargaining power, assured that the employer's initial offer will come in on the high end, and determined your negotiating priorities. Now it's time to time to talk money—and maybe a few perks. Ideally, the offer will come at just the right time—after you've had enough discussion for the employer to get to know and respect you, and for you to get a good reading on the job, the company, your manager, and your colleagues. If you're in the enviable position of Most-Wanted Candidate, though, the offer may come too soon, before you're certain the job suits you and the employer recognizes its full value. In this case, you can discourage a premature offer with a conversation like this:

Manager: I've looked over your resume, and from what you've done, I feel you'd do well in the finance manager job. We can offer you $75,000 a year, with a $5,000 starting bonus. How does that sound?

You: Well, we really haven't talked much about the job and how it relates to your success. Could we start there?

Sometimes the opposite happens—discussions seem to go on and on, yet no offer is forthcoming. Maybe there's some nagging concern they have about you, and they're reluctant to address it directly. Maybe they can't agree on the necessary qualifications. Maybe their business has taken a dive, and they won't confess it to an outsider. Maybe they're hoping for a miracle person to walk through the door, and you're the fallback candidate. In this situation, if you really want the job, just go for it:

Manager: Nice to see you again, Ellen. People say they enjoyed meeting you.

You: Thank you—that's good to hear. I hope you won't think I'm being pushy, but I really would like to know if there's a job offer forthcoming. While this job is particularly appealing to me, I do have several other prospects, and I need to know how to allocate my time.

Manager: Oh, yes. We're serious. We just want to be sure everyone has met you and that we feel comfortable that it's a good fit—for your own sake, as well as ours.

You: Can you give me an idea of why you're not sure if I'm the right candidate?

Manager: Well, one or two of my people are worried that you don't have an engineering background and might not relate well to such a technical product.

You: I'm glad you brought that up, because I think I can satisfy their concerns. I worked in an electronics lab part-time during the year I graduated, so engineering thinking comes naturally to me. And although my degree is in oceanography, I studied physics and chemistry as well—I have a general science background. Is that helpful?

Manager: Yes, very much so. I think we're prepared to go ahead. I'll have an offer drawn up for you.

It doesn't matter whether you get the initial offer verbally or in writing—in many cases a verbal offer is a natural development—but you should never negotiate aggressively before you have a written offer in hand. Verbal agreements are much easier than written ones for an employer to back away from either before or after you've taken the job. If the employer doesn't volunteer an offer letter, politely ask for the offer in writing, so that you can give it careful consideration.

Copyright 2003 WetFeet, Inc.

Taking Stock

Now's the time to go back to the decision matrix you created earlier. Based on the additional knowledge you've gathered—interviewing with more firms, finding out more about your top choice—do you want to change the weighting on any of your decision factors or introduce new ones?

The decision factors you settle on should dictate your negotiating priorities. There's no sense in negotiating for something that's of little value to you. If you're a workaholic, why ask for more vacation time? Maybe child-care assistance or overtime pay would be more useful to you.

Next, take stock of where you stand with all your prospects. Is the job you're now negotiating on your top choice, or is there another opportunity you'd prefer? Is this your only job offer so far? Are there others in sight, or have all your other prospects fizzled?

If you're blessed with lots of prospects or have just started your job search, you're in a stronger bargaining position, and you may want to go for more money and some nice-to-have factors. If this is your only serious prospect and you've been looking for a while, you might want to proceed with care. Keep in mind, though, that a thorough job campaign may not produce many offers at the outset but tends to yield multiple offers later on, when all the contacts you've made and meetings you've had start to bear fruit.

Tactics

Selecting Your Response

You've received an initial offer. Maybe it's everything you want—even beyond your expectations. You'd be happy to accept it as is, right now. Our recommendation: Resist the temptation. You don't want them to think they were too generous. You might indicate that you're generally pleased with the offer, but would appreciate an early performance review, tuition reimbursement, or some other extra that won't be a deal breaker. This will leave your manager thinking he or she offered you just enough, but not too much. Once your final request is settled, you sign and prepare to start working.

But even if you've made all the moves designed to produce a superior initial offer, chances are there will be some gap between what you're offered and what you want. (All that effort at impressing your future employer has also boosted your own estimation of your worth!) Here's where serious negotiation is needed. Let's start by considering the effectiveness and appropriateness of various potential responses to the offer.

Responses Based on Your Own Needs

- "I really need to start several hundred dollars a month higher to be able to make my rent payments."

- "Child care is expensive, as you know. Could you include an allowance for that?"

- "I plan to go to night school in the fall, so I'll have to drop my part-time job. I'm afraid what you've offered won't make up the difference."

- "I have an hour-and-a-half commute, so my transportation costs will be substantial. I had hoped you would be able to pay somewhat more than what I've already been offered by a company near where I live."

Tactics

Do these pleas make you want to reach for your wallet? Probably not. The hiring manager is also unlikely to be moved and will probably say something along the lines of "Well, maybe you'd better look for a job that pays better" or "I guess you'd better take that other job, then."

Even if you're in a strong bargaining position and the employer doesn't want to lose you, you've probably shortchanged yourself by requesting coverage of a specific, relatively small item, rather than asking for more based on your perceived worth.

This kind of approach can be useful, however, in winning a specific item after you've used more fruitful approaches to achieve your main compensation objectives. Here are a couple of examples of how this can work:

- "Now that we're in agreement on salary and bonuses, I'd like to bring up one other matter. I have a fairly lengthy commute every day, and want to be able to put in the hours here that the job requires. This will mean some child-care expense that I wouldn't have with a job closer to home. Can you include an amount to cover these costs?"

- "I have only a few units left toward completing my master's degree, but I'll need some daylight hours to do it. Could I compensate for being away at class one morning a week with some evening work, and would you be willing to provide tuition reimbursement?"

Note that in both of these examples there's an implicit advantage to the company in granting the request: your ability to put in long hours, or your ability to apply knowledge obtained in completing a master's degree.

Responses Based on Data

- "I realize that every company is different, but my review of data on compensation for IT systems analysts at local companies employing more than 500 people suggests an average compensation about 10 percent higher than what you've offered and an upper end about 20 percent higher. I know you want to get the best talent . . ."

- "From what you've told me, the financial analyst job is really a consulting position, not just an accounting position. A good financial analyst, which I think I am, can save the company hundreds of thousands of dollars a year. I hope you can manage a salary for me that's more in line with consulting—and which I believe would be a fair amount higher than what you've offered."

- "I believe the salary you've suggested would place me at the most junior level in the department, paywise. I realize that you're not yet directly familiar with my work, but you apparently spoke with my references, and I'm sure you found out that I learn quickly and do high-caliber work. Could you improve on the offer, taking these factors into account?"

These approaches are good bets to get you an improvement on the initial compensation offer, and you can then make a counterproposal. This is a much better approach than countering right away, which puts you in the position of haggling, and deprives you of the opportunity to "coach" the company to an even higher number. For example:

Employer: (Improving on a first offer of $60,000) Well, I guess that given your qualifications and excellent recommendations, we could stretch and go to $66,000.

You: (Coaching) Thank you for making allowances for my background and experience. And your new offer does bring us closer to what I think would be fair and acceptable—$72,000 . . . (The request for an early review is one you might plan to make if the negotiation seems to be going your way. If you have difficulty getting an increase in the basic salary, this extra request would be pushing it.)

You: (After a few seconds pause, during which the manager does not seem to have had a heart attack) . . . provided we can review my performance in a few months and make an adjustment based on your knowledge of what I can produce.

Responses Based on the Employer's Needs

It's usually more effective to define your needs in terms of benefits to the employer:

- "One thing that occurs to me is that you're hiring me primarily for my skills in running a top-notch kindergarten program. But I know that each additional student means hundreds of dollars a month to the school, and I have ideas for marketing the program to parents of the preschoolers and to real-estate professionals. I know I could pursue them without interfering with my kindergarten responsibilities. Couldn't we combine the two roles and come up with a great solution for both of us?"

- "My computer graphics and communications skills will certainly help me in my role as a customer service representative. But I believe our procedures manuals could benefit from a simplification. From what I've been hearing, they involve some paths that are no longer relevant and others that are hard to understand. I know you don't have a lot to spend on getting external help on this, but I'm qualified and would be glad to help when time permits. I think this would be of value and possibly justify a higher salary."

- "One way out of this dilemma might be for me to take on operations management of the Opal-lite project as a short-term assignment. Then, when I've had the opportunity to demonstrate that I can get things moving and develop procedures to keep them from getting off-track again, we could come back to discussing what kind of permanent position I could fill here."

This kind of response is particularly effective with entrepreneurial or otherwise innovative managers. It suggests a way around a salary impasse, rather than getting into a numbers war. Your effort to understand and satisfy the company's needs enhances your perceived value, opening up the negotiating possibilities considerably.

Responses Based on Finding Creative Alternatives

Often a hiring manager really wants to satisfy you, but faces constraints that are impossible to overcome. For example:

- The maximum salary authorization is set in stone by the hiring manager's supervisor or the CFO.

- The company has never paid a moving allowance, and it isn't about to begin now.

- Your request for flextime will open up a can of worms within the department—half the current staff members have asked for it and been turned down.

In situations like these the manager will probably tip you off with language such as "Look, I'd really like to be able to give you what you ask, but my hands are tied," or "That's really all I can do. I just can't go any further. I hope you decide to accept." Then it's up to you to accept, decline, or get creative. Try to find out what the constraint is; then think of a way to bypass it:

- You asked for a salary higher than the manager could offer, but a performance bonus or an early review with a predetermined raise tied to defined goals might net you close to the same amount.

- You asked for a moving allowance, but you could use a signing bonus to cover those costs.

- You asked for flextime, but maybe you could solve the problem by working at home during specified hours.

The dialogue might go like this:

You: So $55,000 isn't a target cap; it's set in stone and there's no way you can pay more?

Manager: That's right. So if you won't take less than $60,000, I don't see how we can hire you.

Tactics

You: Well, the starting salary isn't as important as the opportunity. Would you be able to revise the salary more easily later if I meet the goals you and I discussed?

Manager: Yes, I could do that.

You: Then maybe we can agree on a three-month evaluation, and if I hit the targets we set, we can celebrate by giving me a raise.

Manager: Okay. That's a good way to handle it. Are there any other items we need to cover?

Sometimes the manager will resist your suggestion; if so, try extending your time frame:

Manager: I think that's too soon for us to conclude that your work merits a raise; we're hiring you to do good work in the first place.

You: I certainly intend to do good work, but I hope that you could at least feel comfortable evaluating me within six months. Would that be acceptable?

Manager: Yes, I could agree to that.

If the manager turns down your request because it's "just not done here," but you have an example to the contrary, try a diplomatic response like this: "Perhaps I was misinformed or don't fully understand the situation, but I was told that Julie Parker did receive some help with her move from Colorado Springs. Maybe we could use a similar justification?" This allows the manager to concede that there are special cases—without having to admit to having mis-represented the situation.

Responses Designed to Create Anxiety

In somes cases, you can use simple techniques to make the hiring manager uncomfortable enough to make him or her give you more than originally intended. Anxiety can work in your favor, but be careful. The idea is to create tension that can work in your favor without overdoing it. If you carry this tactic too far, it'll backfire. Here are some examples of where the technique worked:

- The manager makes an offer of $49,000. You look unhappy and wait 15 seconds without giving any verbal response. Chances are good that the manager will feel anxious and say something like: "I could maybe go a little higher—say, to 51 or 52." (When's the last time you made $3,000 just for shutting up? Sometimes anxiety on the manager's part can work in your favor, but don't overdo it.)

- The manager, who you know has invested several months in the hiring process, has finally settled on you and hopes you can begin immediately. She makes an offer of $85,000. You ask for a few days to think it over. She asks if the salary is the issue. You say that it's certainly a factor. She ups the offer to $90,000, provided you give her an answer now and agree to start Monday. (The advisability of further negotiation depends on the strength of your bargaining position. If it's relatively weak, don't push your luck. But if you know it's strong, you could name a slightly higher figure that would settle the salary issue for you and still leave other areas open for negotiation. Or you could agree to the $90,000 and bring up a signing bonus.)

- The manager makes an offer of $75,000 plus 5,000 stock options. You say how excited you are about the company and its prospects. You say the offer is appealing, but a little less so financially than one you received just a couple of days ago from another start-up. The manager asks about the gap, and you disclose that the base salaries are close, but the other company is about twice as generous with its options and has similar prospects. The manager asks to compare what the options are really worth and then increases the offer to 8,000 options, plus 2,000 more for each year you stay with the company. (Worth the anxiety you created—unless you invented the other company and the manager invites you to take its offer.)

Tactics

Do not confuse anxiety-producing approaches with hostility. You should be extremely courteous at all times, particularly when you are talking about a competitive offer or delaying. Take this example:

You: Thank you very much for your offer. You've made it really difficult for me. I'm eager to work here, and I've heard only good things about your department. But financially, this just isn't as attractive an offer as I hoped it would be. On Monday I received an offer from another great company that's somewhat higher. I'll have to get back to you on this.

Manager: Tell me more about the other situation. Maybe we can find a way to do a little better. . . .

Responses Designed to Reduce Tension

If you feel like the tension is growing out of control and the hiring manager is on the verge of turning hostile, it's time to back off:

- "Maybe I'm being a little unrealistic about what you can do. If so, I apologize. I really want to work here, and I'm just hoping to reach an agreement that seems fair to you and takes into account what I bring to the job."

- "I noticed your reaction to what I just proposed. Maybe that's more than you can do, so perhaps you could tell me what is possible." (It's better to invite the person to name a number that's more acceptable than to underbid yourself by suggesting a reduced amount and then have to keep backing off. You'll soon look pretty foolish.)

- "I hope I'm not giving you the impression that I'm not committed to the company. The only reason I asked for all 10,000 right away is the way this company is exploding. Can't we work it out so that I'm awarded the 10,000 shares now, but only 2,500 vest now, and the rest vest over three years? That way you'll have a completely motivated employee right away, instead of one who hopes the price of shares doesn't go up too much!" (Note that this proposal locks in the share price at today's value.)

Prepare to Change Your Approach

Some negotiations are concluded in a single meeting. Others may stretch out over a few days and involve several players. You're likely to face many twists and turns in the negotiating process, and you should be prepared to change your approach to suit the situation.

Rushing the discussions could force you to agree to less than you might otherwise achieve or prevent you from receiving a competing offer, which would strengthen your bargaining position. Delaying the discussions, on the other hand, leaves an opening for another strong candidate to appear, reducing your bargaining power.

This is why you need to constantly assess your bargaining power. Remember: If you reach for the stars and your ladder is only moon-high, you risk being seen as too demanding or too high-maintenance. If you don't reach at all, you're almost certainly passing up money and benefits the employer would have been willing to grant. And if you know you're seen as a must-have, you can be bold—but never be arrogant. That will only make them want you less. Instead, go to extra lengths to express gratitude for the offer, even when saying no to an inadequate proposal, and suggest that you'll think about what might work better.

Tactics

The Employer's Bag of Tricks

The hiring manager probably has some experience in negotiating, and may be adept at tactics designed to get you to accept an offer or conditions that aren't exactly what you had in mind. Let's take a look at some of the more common tactics.

Imaginary Competitors

The hiring manager or recruiter may drop hints that your requests are becoming too onerous, and that there is another candidate—or even several—waiting in the wings. This may be true, and in that case you should take heed. Or it may just be a ploy to win your quick acceptance. There's no sure way to tell, but you can inquire about the other person's qualifications. If the person is real, you're likely to get a description, which will allow you to make a value comparison. If the person is a phantom, you'll probably get a vague answer. Depending on your reading of your current bargaining power, you can continue negotiating or accept the offer as final and proceed accordingly.

Delays

You may be jubilant over a series of excellent interviews at Company X and the promise of an offer in the mail. The offer is slow in coming, however, and when it arrives, it's less than you expected. You communicate with the person who sent you the offer and request a meeting. The meeting takes a while to arrange, and then it's postponed. You are getting anxious and may be tempted

to accept the meager compensation in the offer letter. Delays can occur for a variety of reasons, and it's not always easy to tell what's going on in a particular situation:

- Something may have changed in the organization's business situation, causing a temporary hold on new hiring.
- Something may have happened that affects the job itself, changing the requirements and the type of person who could best fulfill them.
- The hiring manager may be on the way out.
- Another candidate may have entered the picture.

Regardless of the reason, the best way to deal with delaying tactics without undermining your position is to get busy on your job campaign again. Call those contacts, set up more meetings, put positive energy into the universe. Pretty soon options that are equal to or better than what Company X has put on the table will pop up. Now you have bargaining power, as well as two other fine offers.

Is this really the way the world works? Yes. Job offers tend to come in clusters, if you've been active in setting up meetings, networking, interviewing, and doing everything else that goes into a campaign.

Rushing You to Decision

A manager may tell you he must fill the job this week—take it or leave it. The aim is twofold: to gain your quick acceptance of terms you might not otherwise agree to, and to prevent you from exploring other options and finding something better. While there may be some urgency, it is more than likely exaggerated. Most managers will wait a reasonable time (say a week) for you to consider and discuss the offer—if they truly want you.

Tactics

What can you do to slow things down? Simply say that this is a very important decision and you need a few days to give it the consideration it deserves. This may well result in the manager improving the offer to spur you to an early decision. In this situation you need to consult your decision matrix to get a picture of how this offer compares with your other options. Accept in haste, repent at leisure.

Promises, Promises

Accepting a job is a bit like getting married. During the courtship period, many promises are made. Depending on your partner, they may or may not be kept.

Some managers will deliver on every detail of any commitment they made while recruiting you. Others will make lots of empty promises. What can you do to protect yourself? First, you should ask about the hiring manager's reputation while you are interviewing for the position. You can do this diplomatically by asking neutral questions such as "What do you like best about Tom's management style?" and "What, if anything, do you find not to be as helpful in his approach?" These questions are unlikely to ruffle Tom's feathers if he hears about them—unless he's very insecure, dictatorial, or otherwise difficult to deal with, in which case you don't want to work for him anyway. Managers prone to misrepresenting prospects, impending changes at the company, or other matters can't be trusted on employment commitments. Second, get the important commitments in writing, as part of your final letter offer. After all, even the most trustworthy managers can be reassigned or leave the company, and their verbal commitments won't mean much when they're gone.

Policy

"It can't be done. It's against our policy." This may or may not be true. Very few policies are observed without exception, and your situation could be an exception. Even if it isn't, there are often routes around unmovable policies— you just have to seek them out.

Mind Your Manners

You may get frustrated by the slowness of the process, rescheduled meetings, lack of communication, or brusque responses to your queries. These are indicators of the organization's culture, and you may want to take this into account when deciding whether to accept or reject the offer. But there's never a reason for you to abandon good manners. Politeness will get you favorable attention; rudeness never will.

It's possible to be polite even when you're saying no or insisting on obtaining a clearer picture of what's happening. For example: "Pardon me, but I'm unable to arrange my schedule without knowing when I might be able to conclude my discussions with Mr. Harper. People are calling, wanting to know when I might be available, but I'd like to give Mr. Harper priority. Could you talk with him, please, and let me know whether Monday or Tuesday would be convenient for our wrap-up discussion on the possibility of my joining his department?"

Tactics

Negotiating No-Nos

Employer: Knowing that we don't pay at the top of the industry, why do you want to work here?

You: I really don't need the money. I just like the work. (This may be okay if you're sure others in the work group or the manager are similarly motivated. Otherwise, the manager may wonder how to motivate you.)

Employer: Would $80,000 be a good starting figure?

You: Wow! Wait till I tell my friends! They thought the offer would be much lower! (Keep your cool! Your employer probably knows the typical salary range for a position like this and has made a competitive offer. It does you no good to reveal that you haven't done your homework and that the manager could get you for less.)

Employer: Would $40,000 be a good starting figure?

You: I couldn't manage on that, unless I sold my car, which I'd hate to do, because I need it to come to work. (Will the manager have to give you a raise or a bonus whenever you need to see the dentist, too?)

Employer: I guess that about wraps it up. When can you start?

You: I'm planning to take a vacation in August, and then I'll have some personal business in early September. How about September 15? (Why didn't you bring this up earlier? No one likes surprises from new employees.)

Tactics

Other Mistakes

You: I don't really need this job, so if you don't make it worth my while, I'm not going to take it. (Whoa! This is likely to really push the manager's buttons—the ones that print out the letter revoking the offer. True or not, this statement sounds like a threat. And if you do end up getting the job despite this gaff, you'll have quite a reputation to live down.

You: Since my child is in school, is it possible to take off school holidays? (This is touchy. Be sensitive to company culture when bringing up family responsibilities. If the manager tells you she hasn't taken a day off in two years, you're better off keeping quiet about this and finding a way to make your standard vacation allotment work. But if the salary is low and the company can't pay you more, this may be negotiable.)

Wrapping It Up

- The Decision

- Putting It All Together

- About the Author

The Decision

You've honed your negotiating skills and received a fine offer from Company X. It's decision time. If you've gone this far, this should be a job you want. But is it the job? The answer may not be immediately obvious. If you've been promised an offer within days from Company Y—one that rates considerably higher on your decision matrix, you may want to delay. The choice is tougher if you've just learned of an opportunity at Company Y. Delay may cost you the job with Company X, and you may never get an offer from Company Y. Company X's offer also presents a dilemma if you've just begun your job search and have no idea what else may be out there. Maybe a dream job at Company Z will come up, and maybe nothing else will even compare with Company X's offer.

Consult your decision matrix. If Company X scores 850 or above, it's probably not a bad place to go, unless you are the type who draws on an 18 in blackjack. If Company X scores in the 600s or lower and you're at an early stage of your job campaign, you may want to tell Company X you're not ready to make a decision and let the chips fall where they may. There's a good chance you'll find something better. If you've been looking for a while, this is a tougher call. It's hard to turn down a certain offer on the hope that you'll find something better. And yet, if you've made plenty of contacts and had numerous information meetings, you should eventually come up with an offer that scores above 600. Hold out if you can afford to, perhaps by taking on project work—especially if you can do it at a place you'd like to be on a long-term basis.

If your choice is between two companies rating in the 800s, you'll probably agonize over it. Ask a friend to listen to how you describe both opportunities

and tell you which you seem to prefer. If that doesn't work, try it with another friend. In the end, you can always flip a coin—you probably won't go wrong with either job.

Delaying Your Decision

You're waiting for an offer from Company Y and want to hold off company X. Be reasonable—you can't expect a company to wait a month while you make up your mind. You can usually get a week or ten days of breathing space, though. If all your negotiations so far have been verbal, ask to receive the terms you've agreed upon in writing. It usually takes a few days for everyone involved to sign off on the offer, and you can be "out of town" or otherwise temporarily unavailable when it arrives. Then you can reasonably request a few days to consider the offer, and possibly clarify a few more points. By the time any revisions you agree on are approved and sent back to you again, ten days will have elapsed. If you've received the offer from Company Y by now, make it clear that you're going to have to turn down another offer. Company Y should then proceed with you promptly and in good faith. If Company Y still has not made an offer, you might give one more notice of your need to make an immediate decision. Company Y will either act quickly to make you an offer, convey regret that it can't act more quickly (so if you turn down Company X, it's at your own risk), or wave you off.

Knowing When to Say No

When you've negotiated whatever is possible and the offer still falls short, act decisively. You owe it to the company, which has committed considerable time to you, to phone the manager and relay your decision to pursue other opportunities. You should follow up this call with a letter or e-mail thanking the hiring manager for his or her time and efforts on your behalf. Graciousness

ensures that you will be remembered favorably—you won't burn any bridges. Fail to notify company promptly of your decision, or fail to do so politely, and it could come back to haunt you.

Knowing When to Say Yes

If you don't accept an offer when the time is ripe—when your negotiations have yielded whatever they're going to yield—it may vanish. Once the company concludes that you're impossible to satisfy, it will turn immediately to other options. There's always a backup candidate or a backup plan, and you should keep this in mind before letting a good opportunity pass you by. Especially if a small element of rancor intruded in your final negotiations, now is the time to express your delight at the opportunity to work at such a great company. You want to start your new job with everyone glad to see you, not resentful!

Get It in Writing

Make sure you receive a written offer that notes:

- Your title and major responsibilities
- Your starting date
- The person you'll report to
- Your salary
- Any other forms of compensation, such as bonuses and commissions, what you have to do to receive them
- Any stock options, the dates they will granted, the strike price, and the vesting schedule
- Perks, such as a moving allowance, tuition reimbursement, extra vacation time, flextime, early salary review, or any other special arrangements you agreed on

Wrapping It Up

The offer should be written on company letterhead and signed by the hiring manager or someone else with the authority to commit the company to the terms described. A verbal offer is subject to erosion by reinterpretation, faulty recollection, the desire of the company to elude any special arrangements you managed to negotiate, or the migration of the hiring manager within the company or to another job. And it's worthless in court. A written offer—really a contract, once you've signed it—protects you from backpedaling. If it seems too difficult for the company to prepare such a letter (executives at start-ups, for example, are often too busy to follow up), you can write it yourself and get a senior executive to sign it. Remember, though, that ambiguous language is interpreted to the disadvantage of the person who drafts the contract. Make sure every point is crystal clear if you do the drafting.

You may have already received a written offer from the company. If your negotiations have led to only minor changes, you can simply strike out the language as necessary, write in the changes and initial them, get the person who signed the letter to initial them, and sign and date the agreement. But most companies will prefer to prepare a clean letter with the changes incorporated. Make sure you end up with a signed copy of the final agreement and file it in a safe place.

Version 1

Manager: So how much were you thinking about as a starting salary?

Candidate: I've just become engaged, so I'll need a bigger apartment. And we're thinking of starting a family after the wedding. So I need $55,000 to begin with, plus a health plan. (Remember, never be the first to name a figure. And, in any case, personal needs aren't good persuaders, especially when they raise concerns about competing interests.)

Manager: We've never paid anything like that to a beginner! I'm afraid we just aren't speaking the same language.

Candidate: Well, maybe when you were young, families could live on a pittance, but that's not the way I plan to start out. So how much do you think you can afford to pay? (Even without the sarcasm, insult, and pomposity, a strident tone like this is likely to anger the hiring manager; at a minimum, it won't lead to a productive discussion of what you can contribute to the company.)

Manager: (Withdrawing from a relationship that already is souring) I'll have to take it up with my HR people. We'll get back to you. (Probably with a rejection letter.)

Candidate: (Realizing he has said something offensive, but still clueless) I hope you can do some persuading with them. I want to be reasonable, and maybe I could take a little less. . . . (Sorry, pal; it's too late now.)

Manager: (Now focused on getting the candidate to leave) I'm afraid I have another meeting to get to now. We'll get back to you (with a rejection).

Version 2

Manager: So what were you thinking about as a starting salary?

Candidate: I don't know. How about maybe $48,000? (Again, it's a mistake to name a figure in response to this question, and when you do say what you want, make sure you sound like you think you deserve it.)

Manager: (Sounding shocked) We can't possibly pay that much to a beginner. The highest I can go is $38,000. (The manager may not really be shocked; you need to probe more to find if this is really a cap.)

Candidate: (Unprepared for this, and not wanting lose the job) Okay. I hope I can start this coming Monday. (This isn't negotiation. It's capitulation!)

Manager: Good. But I need a little time to check references, prepare an offer letter, and discuss this with my boss. He doesn't always automatically approve paying the top rate and may not go for your limited experience, even though I believe you can do the job. (The manager is surprised that the candidate has accepted—he had reserved some extra money for negotiations. Now the manager is worried the candidate seems anxious and may not be a great prospect after all—time to rethink this.)

Candidate: (Sensing the manager's new reluctance) I can be somewhat flexible, but hope it doesn't go too much below $38,000. (It definitely will now.)

Manager: (Doubtfully) I'll see what I can do.

Wrapping It Up

Putting It All Together

We've looked at an array of strategies and tactics one by one. Now it's time to see how they work together. The following vignette illustrates several key principles. The setup: Ray Larkin is interviewing with hiring manager Dan Greene for a position as circulation manager at Toolchest. Toolchest is a privately held corporation with $14 million in annual revenues. It publishes four trade journals in the construction contracting field.

Ray came in to see Dan through an introduction from a mutual friend, Mark Lewis, who didn't know much about Dan's operation but thought he could help Ray advance his publishing career. Dan has already given a brief presentation on his background and goals, noting his experience as an advertising representative for *The Washington Post* and as business manager for *The San Jose Mercury News*'s website. Dan takes an interest and mentions that he is looking for a circulation manager for his publications. This is their second meeting.

Ray: From the way you describe the circulation manager position, it sounds like you're not satisfied with the circulation figures for either *Master Plumber* or *Master Electrician*, and you think the previous circulation manager took too passive an approach to the job.

Dan: Very much so. We're not reaching a lot of people who should be reading our publications.

Ray: Well, I took the liberty of interviewing six electrical contractors in the San Jose area and several plumbers. They told me they were thirsty for more business-focused material, possibly with a case-history thrust. How to minimize fall-through-the-cracks specifications. How to deal with tough inspectors who

produce new code requirements on an almost daily basis. How to determine whether to buy or rent equipment. That sort of thing. (This demonstrates initiative and solid research skills.)

Dan: I think you're onto something, which is why I'm considering you for the job. I need a circulation manager who will get into the marketplace, and help us identify new trends and interests, as well as get us to a high level of penetration in our markets.

Ray: It would help to know what boosting the circulation for each magazine by 10,000 would mean, considering the impact on advertising space and rates. (This gets Dan to quantify the value of the circulation manager's work.)

Dan: I've worked out that every 1,000 readers means a below-the-line impact of about $15,000.

Ray: So a 10,000 target for each of the two publications would mean big money—$300,000 if my arithmetic is right. And that's annually! I see a lot of things we can do, going well beyond editorial into marketing. Contests. Awards. Trade-named merchandise. Catalog and supplier tie-in deals. If that's a way you'd want to go, I might be interested in becoming your market development manager, responsible for the advertising, marketing, and circulation functions.

Dan: I'd certainly consider any reasonable business proposal. (Note how Ray has established his own credentials, shown the potential value of an enlarged position, and demonstrated that he is a logical candidate for it, encouraging Dan to think about a higher starting salary without even mentioning money!)

Next meeting: Ray has prepared a business proposal and sent it to Dan, who has reviewed it.

Dan: I commend you for the clarity of your presentation, the good ideas, and the financial projections you put together. I think this might, with a few alterations, be a workable plan. And I like the fact that several of these ideas might be applicable to other publications in our Master's series.

Ray: Thank you. I'm glad you think I'm on target.

Dan: You omitted any mention of your salary expectations. Could you give me an idea, please?

Ray: Of course I've thought about it, but I haven't reached any conclusions. Most important, I'm attracted by the opportunity to turn around Master Electrician and Master Plumber. And, there are a lot of possibilities. A performance bonus. Stock options. Salary is only one consideration. What did you have in mind? (Notice how deftly Ray handles the salary expectations question.)

Dan: We had a tough year last year and have to be conservative. But I do see you as a key player in a turnaround. How about $75,000, with a review in six months, depending on results? (Dan was originally thinking $50,000 for a circulation manager, but now that he sees Ray as a market development manager and potentially as a business manager, he's raised the figure significantly.)

Ray: $75,000 might be okay, provided we can tie down the bonus opportunity. Let's say I've raised circulation by 5,000 per publication by August. That would already be worth $150,000 to you. Wouldn't a 20 percent bonus make sense? (This ties the request to his benefit to the company.)

Dan: (Gulping, but following the logic) I think more like 15 percent. I wouldn't want to get the other people on your level stirred up. (A warning signal.)

Ray: I understand. Perhaps the other 5 percent could be in the form of stock options. At a reasonable projection of the worth of the options, I would see

7,500 options, vesting over four years, as a fair amount. (A creative substitution, based on homework on the company's valuation and number of shares outstanding.)

Dan: I've never given more than 3,000 to a new employee, but in your case, I guess I could stretch it to 5,000. And that's going to have to be it. I feel I'm already stretching pretty far! (Strong warning signal.)

Ray: We have a deal then. I'm excited to start work, and I hope to make a major contribution. Can you get me a written offer, please, so I can end my discussions at other companies? (Knows when to say yes.)

Dan: You can pick it up here tomorrow morning. Shall I assume you'll start two weeks from today?

Ray: That'll be fine. I look forward to working with you. (Gracious acceptance and indication of eagerness to begin.)

About the Author

Robert A. Fish, PhD, is an expert on the skills needed to climb the corporate ladder. Over the past 20 years he has personally counseled thousands of executives, managers, and professionals on marketing their talents.

Rob's own career demonstrates his expertise in personal marketing. He founded and heads the consulting firm SageWorks, which provides strategic and marketing advice to companies seeking rapid growth and better bottom lines. Previously, he cofounded Right Management Consultants, Inc., the world's largest outplacement, career-management, and career-transition firm. While there, he developed many of the company's written materials and training programs, and opened offices in several locations.

Earlier, Rob founded and was CEO of a software company that developed decision-analysis products for airlines. And during the Kennedy administration he headed up government studies of major technology issues, such as development of a supersonic transport, satellites for communications and navigation, and remote sensing. He earned his PhD in astrophysics at the University of Chicago and is a graduate of Harvard.

Rob is a regular contributor to WetFeet's Insider Guide series. You'll find more of his easy-to-follow, proven strategies in *Get Your Foot in the Door! The WetFeet Insider Guide to Landing the Job Interview*, a guide to effective communications, and *Job Hunting A to Z: The WetFeet Insider Guide to Landing the Job You Want*, an essential tool for networking, interviewing, and landing a job offer.

Wrapping It Up

WetFeet's Insider Guide Series

Ace Your Case! The WetFeet Insider Guide to Consulting Interviews
Ace Your Case II: Fifteen More Consulting Cases
Ace Your Case III: Practice Makes Perfect
Ace Your Case IV: The Latest and Greatest
Ace Your Interview! The WetFeet Insider Guide to Interviewing
Beat the Street: The WetFeet Insider Guide to Investment Banking Interviews
Getting Your Ideal Internship
Get Your Foot in the Door! Landing the Job Interview
Job Hunting A to Z: The WetFeet Insider Guide to Landing the Job You Want
Killer Consulting Resumes!
Killer Cover Letters and Resumes!
Killer Investment Banking Resumes!
Negotiating Your Salary and Perks
Networking Works! The WetFeet Insider Guide to Networking

Career and Industry Guides

Accounting
Advertising and Public Relations
Asset Management and Retail Brokerage
Biotech and Pharmaceuticals
Brand Management
Computer Software and Hardware
Consulting for Ph.D.s, Lawyers, and Doctors
Entertainment and Sports
Health Care
Human Resources
Industries and Careers for MBAs
Industries and Careers for Undergrads
Information Technology
Investment Banking

Management Consulting
Marketing and Market Research
Non-Profits and Government Agencies
Oil and Gas
Real Estate
Top 20 Biotechnology and Pharmaceutical Firms
Top 25 Consulting Firms
Top 25 Financial Services Firms
Top 20 Law Firms
Venture Capital

Company Guides

Accenture
Bain & Company
Bear Stearns
Booz Allen Hamilton
The Boston Consulting Group
Cap Gemini Ernst & Young
Citigroup
Credit Suisse First Boston
Deloitte Consulting
Goldman Sachs
IBM Business Consulting Services
JPMorgan Chase
Lehman Brothers
McKinsey & Company
Merrill Lynch
Monitor Group
Morgan Stanley